Edmund Goldsmid, George Ritchie Kinloch

The Ballad Book

Edmund Goldsmid, George Ritchie Kinloch

The Ballad Book

ISBN/EAN: 9783744776943

Printed in Europe, USA, Canada, Australia, Japan

Cover: Foto ©Thomas Meinert / pixelio.de

More available books at **www.hansebooks.com**

Bibliotheca Curiosa.

THE

BALLAD BOOK.

Edited by

GEORGE RITCHIE KINLOCH,

AND

Revised by

EDMUND GOLDSMID, F.R.H.S.,

F.S.A. (Scot.)

PRIVATELY PRINTED, EDINBURGH.

—

1885.

THE BALLAD BOOK.

Bibliotheca Curiosa.

THE

BALLAD BOOK.

Edited by

GEORGE RITCHIE KINLOCH,

AND

Revised by

EDMUND GOLDSMID, F.R.H.S.,

F.S.A. (Scot.)

PRIVATELY PRINTED, EDINBURGH.

1885.

THE BALLAD BOOK.

I.

The Widow o' Westmoreland.

There was a widow in Westmoreland,
  And she never had a child but ane ;
And she prayed, aye, baith nicht and day,
  She micht keep her maidenhead lang.

"O haud your tongue, my mither dear,
  And say na mair to me,
For a jolly young man o' the king's life-guard,
  My maidenhead's tane frae me."

"Awa, awa, ye ill woman,
  Some ill death mat ye dee !
If a jolly young man o' the king's life-guard,
  Your maidenhead's tane frae thee."

A

But she is on to her true-love gane,
   As fast as gang cou'd she ;
Says, " Gie me back my maidenhead,
   For my mammy sair dings me."

He's buskit her, and he's deckit her,
   And he's laid her on her bed ;
He laid her head whare her feet was afore,
   Gied her back her maidenhead.

He buskit her, and he deckit her,
   Wi' a rose in ilka han' ;
And bade her come to Saint Mary's kirk,
   To see his rich weddan.

Now she is on to her mither gane,
   As fast as gang cou'd she ;
Says, " I'm as leal a maiden, mither dear,
   As that night ye bore me."

" He buskit me, and he deckit me,
   And he laid me on his bed ;
He laid my head whare my feet war afore,
   Gaed me back my maidenhead.

" He buskit me, and he deckit me,
   Wi' a rose in ilka' han' ;
Syne bade me come to Saint Mary's kirk,
   To see his rich weddan."

"O never on fit," her mither said,
  "But on hie horse ye sal ride;
And four-and-twenty gay ladies
  Sal a' walk by your side."

"O wha is this," the bride she cried,
  "That comes sae hie to me?
Is this the widow's dochter o' Westmoreland
  Wha gaed hame and told her mammie?

How could she do't, how did she do't,
  How could she do't?—for shame!
Eleven lang nichts I lay wi' a man,
  But never told that to ane."

"If eleven lang nichts ye've lain wi' a man,
  My bed-fellow ye'se never be;
I'll tak the Widow's dochter o' Westmoreland.
  Wha gaed hame and told her mammie."

II.

The Sleepy Merchant.

THERE cam a merchant to this toun,
I wat he was a clever loon,
And at the door as he stood boun,
  He chappit and cam in:
    He called for a bonnie lass,   (*Ter.*)
  He cou'dna lie his leen.

The merchant's bed it was weel made,
And the merchant lad in it was laid,
A dram for him she did provide,
    Bade him drink and lie down ;
       For ye are the sleepy merchant,   (*Ter.*)
    That canna lie your leen.

And whan the sun it was weel up,
The lassie startit to her feet,—
" I am as leal a maiden yet,
    As I lay doun yestreen :
       For ye're but a sleepy merchant,   (*Ter.*)
    That canna lie your leen."

And whan the breakfast it was by,
Fareweel to her, was a' he could say,
Fareweel to her, was a' he could say,
    But I will come again :
       For he was a sleepy merchant,   (*Ter.*)
    That couldna lie his leen.

And whan the market it was oure,
To that same house he did repair,
And at the door as he stood there,
    He chappit and cam in :
       He called for the bonnie lass,   (*Ter.*)
    That lay wi' him yestreen.

The merchant's bed it was weel made,
And the merchant lad in it was laid,
A dram for him she did provide,

Bade him drink and lie down:
 " For ye're but a sleepy merchant, (*Ter.*)
Ye canna lie your leen."

Atween the bowster and the wa,'
I wat he quickly toom'd it a',
I wat he quickly toom'd it a',
 And syne sat up and sang:
 " Come to your bed, my bonnie lass, (*Ter.*)
I canna lie my leen."

And lang before the brak o' day,
Richt kindly to him she did say,
Richt kindly to him she did say,
 " Pray, tell to me your name ?"
 " Ca' me the sleepy merchant, (*Ter.*)
That canna lie my leen."

" But fesh* ye ben the cradle plaid,
And I'll gie ye a braw new faik,†
Be sure ye dinna let them see't,
 Till I gae frae the toun:
 For they'll mock ye wi' the merchant, (*Ter.*)
That ye lay wi' yestreen."

And whan the breakfast it was bye,
Unto her comrades she did say,—
" Braw news I hae to tell the day,

---

   * *Fesh*—Fetch.
† *Faik*—a checked plaid usually worn by shepherds.

Sin the merchant's gane frae toun :
  For I hae got a braw new faik,
    And frae my merry merchant lad, (*Bis.*)
That I lay wi' yestreen."

But whan she gaed but to fesh it ben,
Behaud what follow'd after then,
There was naithing but the cradle plaid,
  Wi' the tows that tied the same :
    " Foul fa' ye for a merchant,
    Ye're but a cheating merchant,   (*Bis.*)
Ye micht hae lain your leen."

Whan twenty weeks war come and gane,
This merchant he came back again,
And at the door as he stood boun,
  He thus begoud and sang :—
    " Mind ye upo' the merchant,   (*Ter.*)
That cou'dna lie his leen ?"

The lassie she sat at her wheel,
The tears cam trickling to her heel ;
Then up and to the door she ran—
  " Ha ! ha ! he's come again !
    Here comes my merry merchant, (*Bis.*)
    Here comes my merry merchant lad,
That wadna lie his leen."

" O my dear, how may this be,
That ye're sae blae aneath the ee,*
That yere sae blae aneath the ee?
   Ye hae na lain your leen.
     Why did ye mock the merchant,   (*Ter.*)
     Ye bear his pack in your wame!"

He's tane the lassie by the hand,
And tied her up in wedlock band,
And now she is the merchant's wife,
   And she lives in Aberdeen:
     For she's married wi' the merchant,(*Bis.*)
     She's married wi' the merchant lad,
   And he needna lie his leen.

---

* It is considered among the vulgar a sure sign of the unchastity of a young woman to have the under eyelid of a blackish or dark-blue colour. Tytler, in "The bonnie brucket lassie," takes notice of this characteristic:

    The bonnie brucket lassie,
     She's blue beneath the een.

And in the old song of "The shearing is no' for you," we observe the proverbial expression—

    Your blue below the ee,
    Whar a maiden shouldna be.

Physicians, however, do not recognise this as a mark of unchastity; but all the *howdies* declare that it is a *breeding sign*. "If under the lower eyelid the veins be swelled and appear clearly and the eyes be something discoloured, it is a certain sign she is with child,

The Magdalene's Lament.

And she, poor jade, withoutten din,
Is sent to Leith-wynd fit* to spin,
Wi' heavy heart, and claithing thin,
   And hungry wame,
And ilka month a well paid skin
   To mak her tame.
      Ramsay.

As I cam in by Tanzie's wood,
 And in by Tanzie's mill,
Four-and-twenty o' Geordie's men
 Kiss'd me against my will.
    Diddle dow, &c, &c.

For ance I was a lady fair,
 And lik'd the young men well,
But now I'm in the correction-house,
 A woful tale to tell !

---

unless, &c.—*Aristotle's Masterpiece.*   *Green* was also a
sign of conception :--
  " Four and twenty belted knights
   Were playing at the chess ;
  Whan out and came her, fair Janet,
   As green as ony gress."
      Young Tamlane.
 * The house of correction formerly at the foot of
Leith-wynd, Edinburgh.

Whan we were in yon tavern-house,
　We liv'd in a good case,
We neither wanted meat nor drink,
　Nor bonnie lads to kiss.

But now I'm in the correction-house,
　And sair, sair do I mourn ;
But now I'm in the correction-house,
　And whipped to my turn.

A wee drap cabbage-kail in a cog,
　A cog and a wee drap burn ;
A wee drap cabbage-kail in a cog,
　And a bodle bap aboon.

But if I were at libertie,
　As I hope to be soon,
I hope to be a married wife
　Whan a' thir days are done.

IV.

Awa wi' your slavery hiremen,
　Sic lads as ye ca' foremen,
They rise by the cock, and claw the kail-pat,
　And that's the knacks o' your hiremen.

B

Awa wi' your mealy miller,
  Awa wi' your mealy miller,
He's married a wife, and he's brocht her hame,
  And canna do nathing till her.

Awa wi' your limey mason,
  Awa wi' your limey mason,
He's married a wife, and he's brocht her hame,
  And he's ne'er put her gown frae lacing.

Awa wi' your blackie sutor,
  Awa wi' your blackie sutor,
He's married a wife, and he's brocht her hame,
  And he's flung the black about her.

But I'm for the ranting gardener,
  But I'm for the ranting gardener,
He pu'd me a flower on Michaelmas day,
  And it's sair'd me aye sin fernyear.

V.

Jock Sheep.[*]

THERE was a knight and a lady bright
  Set a true tryst to the broom;
The tane to meet at twal o'clock,
  The tither true at noon.

---

[*] Jock Sheep is evidently the Scottish version of the English Ballad of "The Baffled Knight, or Lady's Policy," published in Percy's Reliques, which is "given

Whan they cam to the gude greenwud,
    He lichtly laid her doun :--
" O spare me now, kind Sir," she says,
    " For spoiling o' my goun.

Do ye na see my father's castle ?
    It's guarded weel about,
And ye sall hae your wills o' me,
    Therein, and no thairout."

But whan she cam to her father's yett
    Sae lichtly she lap doun ;
She's shut the door, behind her,
    Says, " Whistle o' your thumb !

And whistle o' your thumb, Jock Sheep,
    And whistle o' your thumb ;
Sae stand you there Jock Sheep," she says,
    " And whistle o' your thumb.

You're like a cock my father has,
    He wears the double kaim,
He claps his wings but craws nane,
    And I think ye are like him.

You're like a flower in my father's garden,
    They ca't the marigold ;
And he that wadna whan he could,
    He shanna when he wold.

---

with some corrections from a manuscript copy, and
collated with two printed ones in the Roman
character in the Pepys collection." The English copy
is decidedly inferior in point of humour and fancy.

You're like a steed my father has,
   He's tethered on yon loan ;
He hangs his head out o'er the mare,
   But darena venture on."

He's turn'd him right and round about,
   And swore he'd got the scorn ;
But he's to hae his wills o' her,
   On Monday or the morn.

He's tane a mantle him about,
   Wi' a cod* upon his wame ;
And he's on to gude greenwud
   Like a lady in travelling.

Then word's cum to her father's castle,
   And thro' the ha' its gane,
That there was a lady in gude greenwud
   And she was a-travelling.

She's tane her mantle her about,
   Her key's out oure her arm ;
And she is gane to gude greenwud
   To see this lady wi' bairn.

But whan she came to gude greenwud,
   She saw nae lady there,
But a knicht upon a milk-white steed
   Kaiming down his yellow hair,

---

* Cod - Pillow.

" Ye're welcome here, my dear," he says,
    "Ye're welcome here, my dow;
Sin ye're sae trusty to your tryst,
    My dear ye sanna rue."

He's tane her by the milk-white hand,
    Sae lichtly laid her doon,
And whan he loot her up again,
    Says, " Whistle o' your thumb:

And whistle o' your thumb, fair may,
    And whistle o' your thumb;
Sae stand ye there, fair may," he says,
    And whistle o' your thumb.

Ye said I was like your father's cock,
    He wore the double kame;
He clapt his wings but craw'd nane;
    And ye thoucht I was like him.

Ye said I was like a flow'r in your father's
      garden,
    They ca't the marigold:
And he that wadna whan he could,
    He shanna whan he wold.

Ye said I was like your father's steed,
    Was tether'd on yon loan:
He hung his head out oure the mare,
    But I think he's ventur'd on !"

"O had I staid in my father's castle,
  And sew'd the silken seam !
But sin ye've tane your wills o' me,
  You may conduct me hame."

He's set her on his milk-white steed,
  And took her to the ha';
Nae lord or lady look'd sae blythe,
  As them twa 'mang them a'.*

VI.

The lassie and the laddie
  Gaed out to wauk the mill,
And waly was the weel made bed
  The laddie lay intil.

---

* EPITAPH ON JOCK SHEEP.

Hic conditur Joannes Ovis,
Who, in love matters, was no novice ;
Puellam validè compressit,
As ancient ditty doth express it.

  The above Epitaph was written by a friend, who,
on reading the ballad thought it worthy of such an
accompaniment.

The laddie gaed to bar the door,
  The lassie gaed wi' him,
And ae it cam into her mind,
  Wi' him she wad lie doun.

She's casten aff her petticoat,
  And sae has she her goun,
Atween the laddie and the wa',
  I wat she did lie doun.

Up gat the nakit fallow,
  And ran frae toun to toun,
And there he spied his master,
  Was walking up and doun.

" The cauld's tane me, master,
  The cauld has taken me,
The hire-quean has taen my bed,
  And I am forc'd to flee.

O' I hae serv'd ye seven lang years,
  And never sought a fee,
And I will serve ye ither seven,
  And haud that quean frae me.

It's up the loan o' Charltoun,
  And doun the water o' Dee,
Aud oure the Cairn-o'-mount, master,
  And farder I could flee."

VII.

The Friar.[*]

O listen, and I will ye tell,
　Wi' a falaldirry, falaldirry,
How a Friar in love wi' a lassie fell,
　Wi' a falee and leetee and a lee,
　　tiddle, tiddle, tee.

The Friar cam to the maiden's bed-side,
And asked for her maidenhead.

"O I wad grant you your desire,
If it was na for fear o' hell's burning fire."

"O hell's burning fire ye need have na
　　doubt,
Altho' ye were in I could sing ye out."

---

[*] Can this be one of the squibs, so liberally ful-minated at the Roman Catholic Priests and Friars, during the days of Sir David Lindsay; when they were satyrized as paying more devotion to "marit wyfis" and "lustie maydens," than to their book and psalter? See an English copy of this Ballad in *Durfey's Pills to purge Melancholy*, vol. i., p. 34, under the title of "The Fryer and the Maid."

" O an I grant to you this thing,
Some money ye unto me maun bring."

He brocht her the money and did it down
    tell ;
She had a white claith spread oure the well.

The lassie cries "my master does come,"
The Friar cries " Whar sall I run ?"

" O ye'll dow ye in below this claith,
That ye be seen I wad be laith."*

The Friar cries " I'm in the well,"
I care na though ye war in hell."

Then the Friar cried, with piteous moan,
" O help ! O help ! or else I am gone."

" Ye said ye wad sing me out o' hell,
" Sing yoursel out o' the well."

" If ye'll help me out I will be gone,
Back to you I'll never come."

She helpit him out, and bade him begone ;
But the Friar asked his money again.

---

* *Var.*—O ye will go behind yon screen,
    There by my master ye winna be seen.

    Then in behind the screen she him sent,
    And he fell into the well by accident.

c

" For your money there's na much matter,
To mak you pay for fumbling* our water.

The Friar he gaed up the street,
Hanging his lugs like a new washen sheet.

Then a' wha heard it commend this fair maid,
For the nimble trick to the Friar she play'd.

VIII.

*   \.   *

The beef, and the bacon,
    The capon and the hare,
And a' kin kind o' kitchen,
    Was weel provided there.

In cam Lizzie Ogilvie,
    Wi' her silk-and-worsted goun,—
" Sit about, brave maidens,
    And gie to me some room ;

For there's ten ell in my petticoat,
    And nine into my goun :
Sae sit about, brave maidens,
    And gie to me some room."

---

* Qu. *Drumbling*—i. e. troubling or mudying.

IX.

Earl of Errol.*

O Errol is a bonnie place,
  Into the simmer time;
The apples they grow red and white,
  And the pears they grow green.

And the ranting o't, and the danting o't,
  According as ye ken;
And the thing we ca' the danting o't,
  Is—Errol's na a man!

---

* Gilbert Hay, tenth Earl of Errol, the hero of this singular production, was married at Kinnaird, 7th January, 1658, to Lady Catherine Carnegy, youngest daughter of James, second Earl of Southesk. The tradition of the country is that the lady actually sued her husband for a divorce on the ground of impotency, and that the incidents really took place as detailed in the ballad, but I have been unable to discover the truth of this tradition. The following excerpt, however, from a note on a South country version of this ballad, preserved in Mr. Sharpe's "Ballad Book," bears strong evidence of the truth of the tradition. It is contained in a letter from Keith of Benholm to Captain Brown at Paris, which, after mentioning other news of the day, concludes :—" Lastly, the sadd (and

O Errol's place is a bonnie place,
  It stands upo' yon plain;
But what's the use o' Errol's place?
  He's na like ither men.

" As I cam in by yon canal,
  And by yon bowling green,
I micht hae pleas'd the best Carnegie,
  That ever bore the name.

Tho' your name be Dame Cathrine Carnegie,
  And mine Sir Gilbert Hay,
I'll gar your father sell Kinnaird,
  Your tocher gude to pay."

" If ye gar my father sell Kinnaird,
  'Twill be a crying sin,
To tocher ony weary dwarf,
  That canna tocher win."

---

not lyke heard of in this land amongst eminent per-
sons,) story of the Erll of Errol's impotencie, which is
lyke, being cum to public hearing, to draw deeper
betuix him and Southesk, than is alledgit it hath
done 'twixt him and Southesk's daughter. These are
the meane emergents we are taken up with, whilst
beyond sea empyres are overturning."—*Scone*, 22*d*
Fib. 1659. Errol is situated in the Carse of Gowrie ;
a district famed for the excellence of its fruit.

The lady is on to Edinbrugh,
    A' for to try the law;
And Errol he has followed her;
    His ainsell for to shaw.

O up bespak her sister,
    Whose name was Lady Ann, *
" Had I been lady o' Errol,
    Or come o' sic a clan,
I wad na in this public way
    Hae sham'd my ain gudeman."

Then up bespak a wily lord,
    He spak it wi' a sneer- -
" If it be the length o' five barley-corns,
    A man he will prove here."

" But up bespak Dame Cathrine Carnegie,
    She was na far awa—
" Indeed, my lord, it may be sae,
    If it had awns† and a'."

Errol has got it in his will,
    To choice a maid himsel;
And he has chosen a weel-faur'd may,
    Come in, her milk to sell.

---

* This lady is sometimes called *Jane*; but both names are erroneous. The Earl of Southesk had only two daughters ; the heroine of the ballad, and Elizabeth, who married *first*, James, second Earl of Annandale, and *secondly* David, Viscount Stormont.

† *Awns*—beards of barley.

" Look up, look up, my weel faur'd may,
 Look up, and think na shame ;
I'll gie to thee five hundred merk,
 To bear to me a son."

He's tane the lassie by the han',
 And led her up the green ;
And twenty times he kissed her
 Afore his lady's een.

Whan they war laid in the proof-bed,
 And a' the lords looking on ;
Then a' the fifteen vow'd and swore,
 That Errol was a man.

But thae hae keepit this lassie,
 Three quarters o' a year ;
And at the end o' nine lang months,
 A son to him she bare.

And there was three thairbut, thairbut,
 And there was three thairben ;
And three looking oure the window hie—
 Crying, " Errol's prov'd a man !"

And whan the word gaed through the town,
 The sentry gied a cry—
" O fair befa' you ! Errol, now,
 For ye hae won the day."

" O I'll tak aff my robes o' silk,
  And fling them oure the wa';
And I'll gae maiden hame agane—
  Awa, Errol, awa!"

" Tak hame your dochter, Sir Carnegie,
  And put her til the glen,
For Errol canna please her,
  Nor nane o' Errol's men."

And ilka day her plate was laid,
  Bot an a siller spune;
And three times cried oure Errol's yett,—
  " Lady Errol come and dine."*

And the rantin o't and the dantin o't,
  According as ye ken;
And the thing ye ca' the dantin o't—
  Lady Errol lies her leen.

---

* *Var.*—Seven years the trencher sat,
    And seven years the spune;
  Seven years the servant cried—
    " Lady Errol, come and dine."

X.

The Astrologer.

THERE was a handsome 'Strologer
　In London town did dwell,
For telling maids their fortune,
　There was few could him excell.
　　　　　With my fal, lal, &c.

A pretty maid, as I heard said,
　Unto his lodgings went,
All for to get her fortune read,
　And that was her intent.

In asking for this cunning man,
　Was answered by his maid—
" He's up into his chamber "—
　" Go, call him down," she said.

" If you would read my fortune right,
　I willing would you pay "—
" There's no doubt but I can, fair maid,
　Will ye walk up stairs with me ?"

" I will not walk up stairs with you,
　Nor any man indeed ;"—
And she spoke with as much modesty,
　As if she'd been a maid.

" You may be as nimble as you're able,
  For I have not time to stay;
You may be as nimble as you're able,
  For I'm but a servant may."

" I know your but a servant may,
  I know you're not a maid!
And its time ye were wed, fair may,
  For ye are the ranting blade.

Deny it not, fair may," he says,
  " For I know it to be so,
That you lay with your master,
  Not many nights ago.

Deny it not, fair maid," he said,
  " For it makes your case the worse,
For you got a crown from him last night,
  And you have it in your purse."

XI.

Kempy Kaye. *

KEMPY KAYE is a wooing gane,
　　Far far ayont the sea.
And there he met wi' auld Goling,
　　His gudefather to be, be,
　　His gudefather to be.

" Whar are ye gaun, o' Kempy Kaye,
　　Whar are ye gaun sae sune?"
" O I am gaun to court a wife,
　　And think na ye that's weel dune.

---

* This ludicrous production seems to be a parody
on a passage in the ancient metrical romance of " The
marriage of Sir Gawaine;" of which a fragment is
published in Percy's Reliques. Sir Kaye, for his
unknightly disrespect of the "lothely lady," whom he
so uncourteously anathematised, is here transformed
into her ardent lover; but unfortunately the termina-
tion of their loves remains unknown, as the ballad
breaks off abruptly at the most interesting point. Sir
Kaye, however, appears not to have been terrified at
the "snout" of the lady, or "in doubt" of his kiss;

" An ye be gaun to court a wife,
    As ye do tell to me,
'Tis ye sall hae my Fusome Fug,
    Your ae wife for to be.

" Rise up, rise up, my Fusome Fug,
    And mak your foul face clean,
For the brawest wooer that ere ye saw
    Is come develling,* down the green.

Up then raise the Fusome Fug,
    To mak her foul face clean;
And aye she curs'd her mither
    She had na water in.

for he seems, if we judge from the "extreme unction"
he underwent, to have been literally *glued* to the lips
of the loathesome lady.

Mr. Sharpe, whose opinion on such matters is de-
serving of the highest regard, considers this ballad to
be of Danish extraction, and refers to the *Illustrations
of Northern Antiquities*, p. 311, for a humourous song
of the same nature, called *Sir Guncelin*, translated from
the Kæmpe Viser, by Mr. Jamieson, in which all the
characters are *kemps* or giants. Kempy is the diminu-
tive of " Kemp," a champion or warrior.

* *Develling*—sauntering.

She rampit † out, and she rampit in,
   She rampit but and ben;
The tittles and tattles ‡ that hang frae her
     tail
  Wad muck an acre o' land.

She had a neis upon her face,
   Was like an auld pat-fit:
   Atween her neis bot and her mou,
Was inch thick deep o' dirt.

She had twa een intil her head,
   War like twa rotten plooms,*
The heavy brows hung doun her face,
   And O! I vow, she glooms.

Ilka hair that was on her head
   Was like a heather cow; †
And ilka louse that lookit out,
   Was like a lintseed bow.*

---

† *Rampit*—pranced about in bad humour.
‡ *Tittles and Tattles*—clots of dirt, such as hang on
a cow's tail.
  * *Plooms*—plums.
  † *Cow*—a twig.
  ‡ *Bow*—the pericarpium of lint.

Whan Kempy Kaye cam to the house,
  He lookit thro' a hole :
And there he saw the dirty drab
  Just whisking oure the coal.

He gied to her a braw silk napkin,
  Was made o' an auld horse brat :
" I ne'er wore a silk napkin a' my life,
  But weel I wat I'se wear that."

He gied to her a braw gowd ring,
  Was made frae an auld brass pan :—
" I ne'er wore a gowd ring in a' my life,
  But now I wat I'se wear ane."

Whan thir twa lovers had met thegither,
  O kissing to tak their fill ;
The slaver that hang atween their twa gabs
  Wad hae tether'd a ten year auld bill.*
    *   *   *   *

* *Bill*—the west country pron. of *bull*.

XII.

Hey the Mantle!*

EARLY in the morning when the cat crew day,
  Hey the mantle! how the mantle!
Our gudeman saddl'd the bake-bread, and fast
    rade away,
  And hey for a mantle o' the gude green hay.

Our gudeman's gane awa to the Mers,
  Hey the mantle! how the mantle!
Wi' his breeks on's head, and his bonnet on's arse,
  And hey for a mantle o' the gude green hay.

---

* Among the numerous ancient ditties enumerated
in the "Complaynt of Scotland" there occurs, *Fayr
luf, lent thow me thy mantil, joy!* "The original song,"
says Dr. Leyden, "is probably lost; but a ludicrous
parody, in which the chorus is preserved, is well known
in the south of Scotland. It begins,
"Our Guidman's away to the Mers,
  Wi' the mantle, jo! wi' the mantle, jo!
Wi' his breiks on his heid, and his bonnet on his ——
  Wi' the merry, merry mantle o' the green, jo!
The Editor has never seen the above version, but
the following one is still preserved in the north
country. Our ancestors appear to have been very
fond of the ludicrous, many specimens of their talents
for that species of composition will be found in the
present collection.

And as he gaed through thick wud, thin wud's
    brither,
  Hey the mantle! how the mantle!
Ilka tree stood a mile frae the ither,
And hey for a mantle o' the gude green hay.

As he cam bye the mill door, he heard psalms
    singing,
  Hey the mantle! how the mantle!
As he cam bye the kirk door, he heard the meal
    grinding,
  And hey for a mantle o' the gude green hay.

There war four-and-twenty tailors riding on a snail,
  Hey the mantle! how the mantle!
"Ho!" quo' the foremost, "I'll be heads oure
    her tail,"
  And hey for a mantle o' the gude green hay.

There war four-and-twenty tailors riding on a
    paddock,
  Hey the mantle! how the mantle!
"Ho!" says the foremost, "we'll haud her at
    the gallop,"
  And hey for a mantle o' the gude green hay.

There war four-and-twenty tailors playing at the
    ba',
  Hey the mantle! how the mantle!
Up started headless and took it frae them a',
  And hey for a mantle o' the gude green hay.

XIII.

FOUR-AND-TWENTY cripple tailors, riding on a
    snail;
  This lies leal on my thrawn sang,
"O," says the foremost, "we'll a' be oure the
    tail,
  And we'll a' be thrawn as we gang O."

Four-and-twenty blind men playin' at the ba':
Up cam the foremost and took it frae them a'.

Four-and-twenty young maids swimming in a pool ;
"O," says the youngest, "we'll a' be drown'd or
    Yule."

Four-and-twenty auld wives skinning at a whale,
Up cam the foremost, and took it by the tail.

Four-and-twenty dirten brats pelting at a frog;
Up cam the foremost, says, "wha's the greatest
    rogue.

Four-and-twenty windmills running in a burn;
By cam the fairies and garr'd them a' turn.

Four-and-twenty young men wi' faces like the
    moon,
Let ony ane do better, for noo my sang is dune.

XIV.

The Man in the Moon.*

I SAW the man in the moon,
  Wha's fou, wha's fou?
I saw the man in the moon,
  Wha's fou, now, my jo?
I saw the man in the moon,
  Driving tackets in his shoon ;
And we're a' blind drunk, bousing jolly fou, my jo.

---

* The above ditty, particularising various optical
illusions, and strange absurdities, to which a man in
his cups is subject, through the medium of seeing double,
reminds us of the eccentricities of the "drunken *menyie*
of old Sir Thom o' Lyne :"—
  Jock looked at the sun, and cried "fire, fire, fire ;"
  Tom stabled his keffel in Birkendale mire ;
  Jem started a calf, and halloo'd for a stag ;
  Will mounted a gate-post instead of his nag :
    For all our men were very, very merry,
      And all our men were drinking.
  There were two men of mine,
  Three men of thine,
  And three that belonged to old Sir Thom o' Lyne ;
    As they went to the ferry, they were very, very
      merry,
    For all our men were drinking.

F

I saw a sparrow draw a harrow,
Up the Bow and down the Narrow,
And we're a' blind drunk, bousing jolly fou, my jo.

I saw a pyet haud the pleuch,
And he whissel'd weel eneuch;
And we're a' blind drunk, bousing jolly fou, my jo.

I saw a wran kill a man,
Wi' a braidsword in his han';
And we're a' blind drunk, bousing jolly fou, my jo.

I saw a sheep shearing corn,
Wi' the heuck about his horn;
And we're a' blind drunk, bousing jolly fou, my jo.

I saw a puggie wearing boots,
And he had but shachled cutes;
And we're a' blind drunk, bousing jolly fou, my jo.

I saw a ram wade a dam,
Wi' a mill-stane in his han';
And we're a' blind drunk, bousing jolly fou, my jo.

I saw a louse chace a mouse,
Out the door, and round the house;
And we're a' blind drunk, bousing jolly fou, my jo.

I saw a sow sewing silk,
And the cat was kirning milk;
And we're a' blind drunk, bousing jolly fou, my jo.

I saw a dog shoe a horse,
    Wi' the hammer in his a—e;
And we're a' blind drunk, bousing jolly fou, my jo.

I saw an eel chase the deil,
    Round about the spinning wheel,
Abd we're a' blind drunk, bousing jolly fou, my jo.

XV.

The Shoemaker.

" Shoemaker, shoemaker, are ye within?
    A sal a falladdie fallee;
Hae ye got shoes that will fit me so trim,
    For a kiss in the morning early?"

" O fair may come in and see,
    I've got but ae pair, and I'll gie them to thee
    For a kiss in the morning early."

He's tane her in behind the bench,
    And there he has fitted his own pretty wench
    With a kiss in the morning early.

Whan twenty weeks war come and gane,
    This maid cam back to her shoemaker then,
    For a kiss in the morning early.

" O," says she, " I can't spin at a wheel,"
" If ye can't spin at a wheel, ye may spin at a rock,
  For I go not to slight my ain pretty work
    That was done in the morning early."

Whan twenty weeks war come and gone,
This maid she brought forth a braw young son,
  For her kiss in the morning early.

" O says her father, we'll cast it out,
  It is but the shoemaker's dirty clout,
    It was got in a morning early."

" O says her mother, we'll keep it in,
  It was born a prince, and it may be a king,*
    It was got in a morning early."

Whan other maids gang to the ball,
She must sit and dandle her shoemaker's awl,
  For her kiss in the morning early.

Whan other maids gang to their tea,
She must sit at hame and sing balillalee,
  For her kiss in the morning early.

---

* *King Crispin* I presume.

XVI.

The Maiden's Dream.

ONE nicht as I lay on my bed
    With all my joys in extasie,
And naething but my maidenhead
    Was for to bear me companie.

One cam to me, both tall and young,
    And unto me great love did show ;
My yielding heart consented straight,
    Then love in every vein did flow.

He talk'd to me of a married life,
    And then bade me appoint the day ;
My yielding heart consented straight,
    I had na power to sae him nae.

And whan the happy morning cam,
    I thocht how bless'd a maid was I,
To see me go along the streets,
    Wi' my bride-maidens in clean array.

And whan to church I was brought then,
    In cam to me my sweet bridegroom—
But friends believe me, sair it griev'd me,
    When I found it was but a dream !

And whan to dinner I was set down,
  At the table-head wi' mickle pride,
To see the smiling bowl gae round—
  "Here's a health to you, my bonny bride!"

And after dinner I was conveyed
  Into a large and spacious hall;
For there the sweetest music play'd,
  Till we did for nicht-bouer call.

And whan to bed I was brought then,
  In cam to me my sweet bridegroom:
But friends believe me, sair it griev'd me,
  When I found it was but a dream!

I wish my dream had lasted long,
  Then I had more delighted been;
But whan I awoke, sair to my hurt,
  Alas! I found it was but a dream!

XVII.

The Covering Blue.

" My father he locks the doors at nicht,
  My mither the keys carries ben, ben;
There's naebody dare gae out, she says,
  And as few dare come in,
  And as few dare come in."

" I will mak a long ladder,
  Wi' fifty steps and three,
I will mak a lang ladder,
  And lichtly come doun to thee.

He has made a lang ladder,
  Wi' fifty steps and three,
And he has made a lang ladder,
  And lichtly come doun the lum.

They had na kiss'd, nor lang clappit,
  (As lovers do whan they meet)
Till the auld wife says to the auld man, —
  " I hear some body speak.

I dreamed a dream sin late yestreen,
  And I'm fear'd my dream be true,
I dream'd that the rattens cam thro' the wa'
  And cuttit the covering blue.

Ye'll rise, ye'll rise, my auld gudeman,
  And see gin this be true,"—
" If ye're wanting rising, rise yoursel,
  For I wish the auld chiel had you."

" I dream'd a dream sin late yestreen,
  And I'm fear'd my dream be true ;
I dream'd that the clerk and our ae dother,
  Wat rowed in the covering blue.

Ye'll rise, ye'll rise, my auld gudeman,
    And see gin this be true,"—
" If ye're wanting rising, rise yoursel,
    For I wish the auld chiel had you."

But up she raise, and but she gaes,
    And she fell into a gin;
He gied the tow a clever tit,
    That brocht her out at the lum.

" Ye'll rise, ye'll rise, my auld gudeman,
    Ye'll rise and come to me now;
For him that ye've gien me sae lang til,
    I fear he has gotten me now."

" The grip that he's gotten, I wish he may haud,
    And never lat it gae;
For atween you and your ae dother,
    I rest neither nicht nor day."

XVIII.

The Muir Hen.

THE bonnie muir hen gaed down the den,
    To gather in her cattle;
I bent my bow to fire at her,
    But I could never ettle.

(Ch.)   *Sing archie owdum diddledum dow,*
     Sing archie owdum dowdum,
     Sing archie owdum diddledum dow dum,
     Diddle dum, diddle dum dow dum.

And ae the nearer that I cam,
  Its ae she sang the louder—
" I loe the young man wondrous weel,
  But they do want the pouder."

" O haud your tongue, fair maid, he says,
  And dinna gie me the scorn;
Ye dinna ken whare we may meet
  Wi' pouder in my horn."

The next time that he did her meet,
  Was doun amang the corn;—
" How do you do, fair maid, he says,
  There's pouder in my horn."

He's tane her by the milk-white hand,
  And on the leys he's laid her,
And there he's tane his wills o' her,
  Before he let her gather.

And when he let her up again,
  And she saw the leys about her;--
" I'll rue the day that ever I said,
  The young men wanted pouder."

Whan twenty weeks war come an gane,
  This maid began to weary;
And ae she cried, " My back, my back,"
  I' the drear time o' the yearie.

And whan he cam into the ha'
   And saw the wives about her—
" Ye're na sae ill's I wish'd ye yet,
   When ye said I wanted pouder.

But I thought my gun would me misgie,
   When I had her on my shouther,
Tho' my flint was soft and fired not,
   'Twas na for want o' pouder."

XIX.

WIDOWS are sour, and widows are dour,
   And widows are aye faint hearted;
But lasses are kind, wi' courtship in mind,
   Wi' money into their pocket.

Money into their pocket, he says,
   And gowd into their coffer ;
But Jeanie Beddie's better than that,
   She has three lads in her offer.

Jamie Jack he loves her weel,
   But Jock Mouat loes her better,
But Willie Anderson will gae mad,
   If that he dinna get her.

Jeanie lay sick on the bleaching green,
   And Willie's leg lay oure her;
He could na get a kiss o' his love,
   For Burley glowring oure her.

"O gin Burley was lying sick,
   And never to get better,
Syne I wad get a kiss o' my love,
   And nane ken o' the matter.

"But gin ye had been wi' me yestreen,
   Ye wad hae riven for laughter,
To see the loun get oure the crown,
   For kissing o' Jeanie Clerk's dochter."

XX.

Bonnie Buchairn.

(Ch.) Quhilk o' ye lasses will go to Buchairn?
    Quhilk o' ye lasses will go to Buchairn?
    Quhilk o' ye lasses will go to Buchairn?
    And be the gudewife o' bonnie Buchairn?

I'll no hae the lass wi' the gowden locks,
Nor will I the lass wi' the bonnie breast-knots,
But I'll hae the lass wi' the shaif o' bank notes,
To plenish the toun o' bonnie Buchairn.

I'll get a thigging frae auld John Watt,
And I'll get ane frae the Lady o' Glack,
And I'll get anither frae honest John Gray,
For keeping his sheep sae lang on the brae.

Lassie, I am gaun to Lawren'-fair,*
" Laddie, what are ye gaun to do there?"
To buy some ousen, some graith, and some bows,
To plenish the toun o' Buchairn's knows.

XXI.

It fell on a morning, a morning in May,
My father's cows they all went astray,
I loutit me down, and the heather was gay,
    And a burr stack to my apron.

O ! ance my apron it was wide,
But now my knees it will scarcely hide,
And O the grief that I do bide,
    When I look to my apron.

O! ance my apron it was new,
But now it's gotten anither hue,
But now it's gotten anither hue,
    There's a braw lad below my apron.

* Lawren'-fair, a market held at Lawrence-kirk, in
Mearns-shire.

I saw my father on the stair,
Kaiming down his yellow hair,
Says—"What is that ye've gotten there,
   Sae weel row'd aneath your apron?"

It's no a vagabond, nor yet a loon—
He's the rarest stay-maker in a' the toun,
And he's made a stomacher to bear up my goun,
   And I row'd it aneath my apron.

I saw my mither on the stair,
Kaiming down her yellow hair,
Says—"What's that ye've gotten there;
   Sae weel row'd aneath your apron?

It is my mantle and my shirt,
I had nae will to daidle it,
I had nae will to daidle it,
   And I row'd it aneath my apron.

As I was walking up the street,
Wi' silver slippers on my feet,
O! aye my friends I'd ill will to meet,
   And my braw lad row'd in my apron.

XXII.

FIRST there came whipmen, and that not a few,
And there cam bonnetmen following the pleugh;
But he was a brisk farmer, he was brisk and airy,
Monie times courted, but never to marry:
    Court her, court her, court her, and leave her,
    O sic a pity that they should grieve her.

The next was a merchantman out o' the town,
She washed his stockings and dichted his shoon;
And aye for the courting the lassie was keen,
The lassie was keen, and the laddie was airy.
     *   *   *   *

XXIII.

Laird o' Leys.

THE Laird o' Leys is to London gane,
    He was baith full and gawdie;
For he shod his steed wi' siller guid,
    And he's play'd the ranting laddie.

---

* This ballad relates to a *faux pas* of one of the
Burnets of Leys, in Mearns-shire; but which of them
I know not.

He hadna been in fair London
  A twalmonth and a quarter,
Till he met wi' a weel-faur'd may,
  Wha wish'd to ken how they ca'd him.

"They ca' me this, and they ca' me that,
  And they're easy how they've ca'd me;
But whan I'm at hame on bonnie Deeside,
  They ca' me the ranting laddie."

"Awa wi' your jesting, Sir," she said,
  "I trow you're a ranting laddie,
But something swells atween my sides,
  And I maun ken how they ca' thee."

"They ca' me this, and they ca' me that,
  And they're easy how they ca' me:
The Baron o' Leys my title is,
  And Sandy Burnet they ca' me."

"Tell down, tell down, ten thousand crowns,
  Or ye maun marry me the morn,
Or headit and hangit ye sall be.
  For ye sanna gie me the scorn."

"My head's the thing I canna weel want;
  My lady she loves me dearlie;
Nor yet hae I means ye to maintain—
  Alas! for the lying sae near thee."

But word's gane down to the Lady o' Leys,
   That the Baron had got a babie;
"The waurst o' news," my lady she said,
   " I wish I had hame my laddie.

But I'll sell off my jointure-house,
   Tho' na mair I sud be a ladie;
I'll sell a', to my silken goun,
   And bring hame my ranting laddie."

So she is on to London gane,
   And she paid the money on the morn;
She paid it down, and brought him hame,
   And gien them a' the scorn.

XXIV.

Tam Barrow.

'Twas in the month of Februar,
   Whan Tam was first a widower;
Thir words I will rehearse to you
   About auld Tam Barrow.

His mukle-coat, his hairy wig,
   O vow! he lookit dreary,
He wad hae put ye in a fricht,
   Gin ance he had cam near ye.

He was na widower lang ago,
  Till he grew tap-and-teerie;
And he has thro' the kintry gane,
  To seek anither dearie.

He wash'd his face, he kaim'd his hair,
  He was a lusty fallow,
And a' the lasses blinkit blythe,
  At auld Tam Barrow.

A' the lasses blinkit blythe,
  But few o' them had tocher,
Na sooner did they gie consent,
  Of them he spier'd their coffer.

But he's to a rich widow gane,
  That hath baith white and yellow,—
" Will ye consent to marry me?"
  Says auld Tam Barrow.

" Your children I will put to school,
  Yoursel I will haud easy;
Ye'll sit richt warm at my fireside,
  Whan you grow auld and crazy."

But he was na married lang ago,
  Till he began to weary;—
" Pack aff your children and begone,"
  Says auld Tam Barrow.

G

XXV.

JOHNIE cam to our toun,
To our toun, to our toun,
Johnie cam to our toun,
The body wi' thet ye ;
And O as he kittl'd me,
Kittl'd me, kittl'd me,
O as he kittl'd me—
But I forgot to cry.

He gaed thro' the fields wi' me,
The fields wi' me, the fields wi' me,
He gaed thro' the fields wi' me,
And doun amang the rye ;
Then O as he kittl'd me,
Kittl'd me, kittl'd me,
Then O as he kittl'd me—
But I forgot to cry.

XXVI.

The Ram of Diram.

As I cam in by Diram,
 Upon a sunshine day,
I there did meet a ram, Sir,
 He was baith gallant and gay.

 (Ch.) And a hech, hey, a-Diram,
  A-Diram, a-Dandalee;
  He was the gallantest ram, Sir,
  That ere mine eyes did see.

He had four feet to stand upon,
 As ye sall understand;
And ilka fit that the ram had
 Wad hae cover'd an acre o' land.

The woo that grew on the ram's back,
 Was fifty packs o' claith;
And for to mak a lee, Sir,
 I wad be very laith.

The horns that war on the ram's head,
 Were fifty packs o' speens;
And for to mak a lee, Sir,
 I never did it eence.

This ram was fat behind, Sir,
 And he was fat before;
This ram was ten yards lang, Sir,
 Indeed he was no more.

The tail that hang at the ram,
  Was fifty fadom and an ell,
And it was sauld at Diram,
  To ring the market-bell.

XXVII.

The Knave.

I GAED to the market,
  As an honest woman shou'd,
The knave followed me,
  As ye ken a knave wou'd.

  (Ch.) And a knave has his knave tricks,
    Aye where'er he be,
    And I'll tell ye bye and bye,
    How the knave guided me.

I boucht a pint ale,
  As an honest woman shou'd;
The knave drank it a',
  As ye ken a knave wou'd.

I cam my ways hame,
  As an honest woman shou'd,
The knave follow'd me,
  As ye ken a knave wou'd.

I gied him cheese and bread,
   As an honest woman shou'd;
The knave ate it a'
   As ye ken a knave wou'd.

I gaed to my bed,
   As an honest woman shou'd;
The knave follow'd me,
   As ye ken a knave wou'd.

I happen'd to be wi' bairn,
   As an honest woman shou'd:
The knave ran awa,
   As ye ken a knave wou'd.

I paid the nourice fee,
   As an honest woman wou'd;
The knave got the widdie,
   As ye ken a knave wou'd.

XXVIII.

THERE was a little wee bridelie,
   In Pitcarles toun,
   In Pitcarles toun;
There was few fowk bidden to it,
   And as few fowk did come,
   And as few fowk did come.

There was nae mair meat at it,
 Than a sheep's head but the tongue: (*bis.*)
And aye the bride she cried—
 I pray ye lads eat some.   (*bis.*)

There was nae drink but a soup
 I' the boddom o' a tun;   (*bis.*)
And aye the bride she cried—
 I pray ye lads drink some. (*bis.*)

There was nae music but a pipe,
 And the pipe wanted the drone: (*bis.*)
And aye the bride she cried—
 I pray ye lads dance some. (*bis.*)

The bridegroom gaed thro' the reel,
 And his breeks cam trodling doun; (*bis.*)
And aye the bride she cried—
 Tie up your leathern whang.* (*bis.*)

The bride gaed till her bed,
 The bridegroom wadna come: (*bis.*)
And aye the bride she cried—
 I kent this day wad come. (*bis.*)

---

* Before the invention of *braces*, the nether garments were usually supported by a leathern belt round the waist.

XXIX.
The Mautman.*

THE Mautman comes on Munanday,
    And vow but he craves sair;—
Now gie me my sack and my siller,
    Or maut ye're ne'er get mair,
      (Ch.) Bring a' your maut to me,
        Bring a' your maut to me;
        My draff ye'll get for ae pund ane,
        Tho' a' my jockies† should dee.

She's tane the chappin stoup,
    And p——d it to the ee——
"O come, gudeman, and prie
    Sic maut as ye've gien me."—

"The maut is very gude maut,
    An' it hadna been brewn sae het,"—
"O how can it otherwise be,
    Whan it's new come out o' the fat. ‡

Now, hark ye, hark ye, kimmer,
    And I will tell ye how
There cam to our house yestreen,
    A curst unruly crew:

* This coarse production is a different, if not an older version of *The Mautman,* published in Herd's Collection.
    † *Jockies*—Pigs?   ‡ *Fat*—vat.

A curst unruly crew,
    And they did breed a quarrel,
They gaed doun to the cellar below,
    And they pierc'd my dochter's barrel:

They pierc'd my dochter's barrel,
    And syne ran awa wi' the cock,
And aye, and aye sin syne,
    My lassie rins lowss † i' the dock.

Some say kissing's a sin,
    But I think its nane ava,
For kissing was won'd * in the warld,
    Whan there was but only twa.

If it wasna lawfu',
    Lawyers wadna allow it :
If it wasna holy,
    Ministers wadna do it.

If it wasna modest,
    Maidens wadna tak it :
And if it wasna plenty,
    Puir fowk wadna get it.

---

* *Lowss*—loose.
| *Won'd*—known, an oblique sense of *dwelt*.

.